FURNITURE RESTORATION AI

By

Cynthia Haas

Foreword

Cindy (Cynthia) Haas began her woodworking career in 1984 in a small shop owned by her and her husband. Over the years she has expanded her knowledge of the trade to include not only repairs, but designing and building her own cabinets and furniture. Cindy's knowledge also includes all types of finishes, veneering, laminates, hand caning, seat weaving and upholstery.

Cindy loves antiques and other beautifully designed furniture and by repairing them she helps to preserve the craftsmanship that defines the pride of our past. In this text she shares with you some of her best techniques to repair valued pieces. By giving you step by step instructions and pictures to accompany them, she hopes you will find them helpful and useful as you undertake your own project.

INDEX

SUPPLIES AND SAFTY STATEMENT, Page 1

LABELING AND DISASSEMBLY, Page 2

CLEANING AND PREPARATION FOR REASSEMBLY, Page 4

REASSEMBLY, Page 5

BROKEN DOWELS, Page 8

REMOVING NAILS AND SCREWS, Page 9

GLUE INJECTION, Page 13

GLUING OR RELAMINATING BROKEN PARTS, Page 14

REPAIRING BROKEN DOWEL ENDS (STEP DOWN DOWELS), Page 16

REPLACING MISSING PARTS OR PIECES, Page 18

REPLACING OR REPAIRING MISSING VENEER, Page 20

TACK RAIL REPAIRS FOR UPHOLSTERED PIECES, Page 22

TOUCH UP FINISHES, Page   23

DO'S AND DON'TS, Page 25

ADDITIONAL PHOTOS, Page 26 - 36

FURNITURE RESTORATION AND REPAIR

Basic Supplies Needed

- Rubber Mallet or a padded club
- WOOD GLUE, not white craft glue, hot glue or epoxies
- Masking tape and a marker pen
- 80, 150, 220 grit sanding papers and/or a wood file
- Drill and drill bits (3/8, 5/16, 7/16 and 1/2 are the most commonly needed)
- Clamps (Rope and a wooden ruler can be used)
- Safety goggles and dust mask
- Paper towels
- Pliers, screw drivers, chisels, Dremel tool and attachments, more tools the better, ice pick or awl, and tooth picks
- Replacement dowels for broken dowels
- White Vinegar

A Flat work surface that's clean and at a comfortable height.

SAFETY FIRST AND FOREMOST, especially with power tools. Read any and all operation manuals for the power tools. Wear safety goggles, dust mask and even a shop apron is a good idea. Take care that all loose clothing and hair is tied securely back out of the area. If you are tired or distracted don't work on your project, that is when mistakes are made and people get hurt.

Sometimes it is the little things that can make the difference between an easy job and a hard one. The two that I have dealt with personally are,

1. "Oh, this is really easy" and sometimes it is, but many times the mistake is, when I think, that I charge into the project and I find I miss seeing things. Then bigger problems come up, so take a few moments to study the project and think about how you are going to proceed.
2. On the opposite end, sometimes I find myself dragging my feet, because I am intimidated by the project. I resolve this problem by going slow, thinking the process through, and sometimes I write a list of steps that I am going to go through to complete the project.

Labeling and Disassembly

To begin, study the object you are regluing, and if any pieces are unattached, dry fit them back into place. Label all parts using the masking tape and marker. (Fig. 1) Make sure that when labeling chair parts you note which rungs or stretchers are on what order from top to bottom, as many times they are different lengths. Be sure to note angles and basic construction of the piece, and look for any nails, or screws holding parts together at this time and remove them. Look for broken dowels and have replacements on hand before beginning. If working on case goods, the back may need to come off at this time to access

Figure 1 Note all parts are labeled, legs, rails, stretchers

interior supports. After labeling and familiarizing yourself with the piece, you can then begin to knock it apart, using the mallet or padded club. A gentle tapping is recommended, although, it can take a hard knock to take furniture apart. If a joint is tight and not yielding, I recommend leaving it alone, unless you actually can feel movement. If too much force is applied you can split the wood and break dowels. If a piece is loose, but not coming apart, clamp it tight to the work area and wiggle it while pulling on it. Sometimes a rotating circular motion works well for chair rungs, or and up and down, side to side movement.

On flat areas, a chisel can be worked in as a wedge while wiggling the piece. (Fig. 2)

When I get the piece apart, I generally lay the pile of pieces together in sections as do not have to be glued back together all at once. For instance I will glue the back of a chair and the front part first, then finish with the side rails. With a chest I glue the end panels

Figure 2 Using a Chisle to work a glue block out. Note even the glue block is labeled,

first then the longer rails. I glue rocking chairs and chairs bases first, then do the upper back and arms. It is important to realize the reason for doing this is the glue grabs quickly and you need to clamp fairly quickly to prevent and glue bond from forming where you don't want it. If something does glue up wrong I have used white vinegar to soak the joints enough to take it apart again, which is why you need to use wood glue.

Cleaning and Preparation for Reassembly

The next step is to clean the old glue off the contact areas, and there are a number of ways to do this. The main goal is to remove glue, not wood. The flat areas and dowels can be cleaned using sand paper or files. Dremels with sanding drums and other bits are great for this. Until you are sure of yourself go slow and be aware that you can chip the edges on the finished piece. All dowel holes and mortise holes need to be cleaned, using drill bits or a Dremel. Be careful not to enlarge the holes. Just remove glue. (Fig. 3)

Figure 3 Filing off old glue. Remove only the glue not wood.

The next step is to make sure that any dowels remaining attached to parts are tight in their holes. If they are not, then using a pair of pliers, wiggle them loose and clean them as well along with their corresponding holes. (Fig. 4)

Figure 4 Checking dowel left in leg for tightness

Reassembly

If you are new to this process, I recommend dry fitting the pieces together first before applying glue to make sure you are getting it put back together correctly. There is nothing more discouraging than having to take a piece apart when glue has been applied. In dry fitting it is not necessary to fit every piece tightly back into place, just familiarize yourself with the fact that these pieces are going where they belong. Chairs in particular can be trick due to the angles of legs into the seat, where stretchers meet legs etc.

Also while dry fitting, this is the time to start thinking about the clamping process, because the clamping process is one of the most important parts of the reglueing procedure, as it forces the glue into the pores of the wood and stabilizes the piece so that the glue bond is secure. It is very important to clamp all pieces tightly and pull all joints flush and tight, right back where the manufacturer had them. Also bear in mind that there should be a barrier between the wood and the metal of the clamps (or ropes) otherwise you can dent and chip edges. I use rubber pads designed for my clamps, but I have also used thin wood or card board. Apply glue to all surface contact areas and in the dowel holes and proceeds to put the piece together again, making sure to clamp all parts tight. (Fig. 5)

If for some reason a joint is not pulling together, take is back apart see if the glue has been forced to the bottom of the dowel hole and is holding it apart, if so use a tooth pick or whatever will fit into the hole remove some of glue. The use your pliers to squeeze a groove down the length of the dowel, this will allow the glue to move up the hole and not pocket at the bottom. Commercial dowels have ridges along them for this reason.

Finally clean off any excess glue, and set the piece, if possible on a flat level area to make sure it is sitting level.

Figure 5 Fully clamped chair, sitting on a level surface.

Sometimes adjusting the clamps can take care of leveling problems. In the index are pictures for different clamping issues.

If the dowel holes are larger than the dowels, I use a mixture of fine saw dust and glue to glue the parts together. If there is a big difference in the dowel holes and the dowels, then the existing dowels need to be replaced with larger dowels and the piece redrilled for the new dowel size. (Fig. 6)

Figure 6 Mixing glue and fine saw dust into a paste to be used in areas where contact points between Parts are not tight.   Dowel holes, mortise joints etc.

Now that I have made this all sound simple, life rarely goes that way and I do have answers for the problems as well, so stay calm and keep reading. Remember, its wood and I have found it can always be repaired or replaced.

Broken Dowels

Broken dowels are probably the most common problem to deal with. The thing to keep in mind is that in cleaning out the old dowels to replace with new dowels, you do not want to enlarge the hole or change the original alignment of the dowel hole from the manufactures original direction.

First secure the piece with broken dowel securely to the work area with a clamp and flush the broken dowel out with the surface with a file so that you can mark the center area of the broken dowel. Use something sharp to make and indentation for a drill bit to sit in. Using a drill bit that is half the size in diameter as the dowel, drill down into the center of the dowel until you feel the drill hit the pocket at the end of the hole. (Fig. 7) You can tell when this happens as the drill is not meeting the resistance of the wood. Then rotate the drill to enlarge the hole you are drilling, so that you leave a thin piece of the dowel in place. The other way is to simply increase your drill bit size until you leave a thin wall of the original dowel in place.

Figure 7 Piece securely clamped to work surface, with a hole smaller than the original dowel hole, drilled down the middle of the broken off dowel.

Then using a small flat screw driver, place the flat end between the broken dowel and the wall of the dowel hole and carefully chip out the old dowel.(Fig. 8) Clean the hole out about a ¼ of an inch to verify the direction of the dowel hole. Using a drill bit the correct size for the dowel hole, finish drilling out the old dowel.

Figure 8 Chip out the thinned out wall of the old dowel using a small screw driver.

Sometimes a broken dowel is loose in the hole, simply drill a pilot hole in the center of the dowel, screw in a screw to act as a handle and pull the broken dowel out. The pilot hole is important. The screw as it's screwed in can cause the dowel to expand and become wedged in place.

Removing Nails and Screws

Nails can be tricky to find, as manufactures use nails to hold pieces together while the glue sets up and then putty over them. First dig out the putty with something sharp like and awl or ice pick. Then drill down with a small drill bit (1/8 of 3/16 in size) on two opposite sides of the nail head. (Fig. 9)

Then using needle nose pliers grab the nail head and lever the nail out. Be sure to put something under the pliers so as not to damage the wood, also be aware many of the manufacture brads/nails are long. Sometimes you have to use the awl or ice pick in the drill holes to wiggle the nail loose. When you finally get the nail far enough out, you can use end cutters or diagonals to grab the nail and finish pulling is out. (Fig.10). If a nail breaks off, repeat the procedure or check to see it you got enough out to finish taking the piece apart.

Figure 9 Two small holes on either side of nail.

Figure 10 Pulling the nail head out with Diagonals, note the wood piece between the chair part and the tool.

Removing screws can be a real pain for various reasons. Sometime they are soft metal and the heads break off or the slots are messed up. I have found that no amount of colorful language will remove them so I use a metal disk cutter on my Dremel and cut a new slot (Fig. 11). When doing this you do sometimes cut into the surrounding wood, it has to be puttied in later. You can also, just create a larger hole and just drill the whole screw out. Screws that have obviously been rusted in place, have responded well to having small holes drilled around their perimeter (3 or 4) and injecting WD40 and allowed the piece to soak overnight. Then I cut a better slot and using a screw driver, I turned them out with a crescent wrench. (Fig. 12)

Figure 11 Cutting a deeper slot in screw head, if possible cut deep enough to cut into the screw shaft.

Figure 12 Crescent wrench allows for leverage on really tight screws.

Another method, is to tap on the screw head with a hammer and screw driver, sometimes it is enough to move the screw in the wood to turn out. Also just drilling off the head of the screw is enough to allow the pieces to come apart, than you can finish turning the remaining screw out with vice grips.

If a screw breaks off and the piece is apart, but the screw is needed to join the piece back together again, then simply drill a new hole angling close to the same areas. There are pictures for most of these circumstances following the text.

Glue Injection

Sometimes a piece of furniture will have only one or two really loose joints and the rest is tight so you cannot do a complete reglue. Sometimes upholstery is attached in ways that you would have to remover everything to do a simple reglue. The looser the piece the better this method is. I find the tools for injecting glue at my local feed and livestock store. I use 20cc syringe and a 14 gauge needle. I cut the flat pointed end off of the needs with end cutter and sand the end smooth, as you can get a really nasty puncture wound. Turn the piece over so that you are working from the underside. Using an one 1/8 inch drill bit, drill a hole at an angle from the joint of the stretcher into the leg until you hit the pocket at the end of the joint, You will feel the drill hit the pocket, as there is no more resistance on the bit. Sometimes a second hole is necessary to release the air in the pocket so the glue has some place to go. Then insert the needle and squeeze. I like to get at least a ½ cc into the joint. Then I plug the hole with a tooth pick and proceed to the next joint. If the parts will allow it wiggle them a little to move the glue around. Be careful when drilling not to twist the drill as the small bits will break off. If that happens just leave it in and start over. Clean off any glue and if there is a lot of movement to the joint, clamp the piece. I have also use screws under piece as well to hold the joint. I don't like to do this as I believe that wood and metal expand and contract a difference rates and that over time this will wear on the piece, and you are removing wood from a joint area. The strength in the piece is from the complete structure of the wood.

Gluing Broken Parts

All broken wood can be glued, it is how the break affects the structure of the piece and where and how the piece is used. Furniture manufacturing regularly glues or laminates wood together to get pieces big enough for turned legs, solid wood table tops, wood panels etc. Many times parts that come apart, are simply where the glue has dried out, especially an old piece that was glued with hide glue. In this case simply sand the old glue off and reglue and clamp the pieces back together. Breaks, whether long or short and jagged, are coated thoroughly with glue and clamped tightly together. A dry run on clamping is important, as on long angled breaks the glue actually lets the parts slip. Be sure parts are flush on all sides as much as possible. In the indexes I have pictures for some of the creative clamping necessary in some cases. In gluing jagged pieces, make sure to remove any pieces that are at angles to the directions of the wood. (Fig.13)

Figure 13 note the angled pieces in the broken wood.

Figure 14 Sliding the broken piece in place from top to bottom, where the jagged edges meet.

In putting these pieces back together, the parts may need to slide together to lock in where the jagged ends are, dry fitting helps with this aspect. (Fig. 14).

On short breaks, after they have been glued, they should be reinforced, as the strength of the wood has been compromised. To do this a piece of wood is cut to fit a mortise made along the break area. Cut the wood so the gain runs length wise I refer to this as a spline. I use two methods to do this. The first and easiest, is a router with a slot cutter and bearing guide. I work from the underside of the piece where I can. Create a spline that matches the wood and grain of the original as much as possible. Never remove more that ½ of the volume of the original piece and branch the break two to three inches on each side of the break. Cut a slot in the broken piece. Pattern out a new piece of wood to fit as tightly as possible, make sure you use the piece running the long grain of the wood for the length of the spline. Glue and clamp the new piece in, leaving some excess on the new piece to sand flush with the old.

If a router cannot access the area, then mark a center line, down the piece as straight and accurate as possible. Drill holes along the line, (Fig. 15) again do not remove more than half the volume of wood of the piece being branched. A one inch by one inch leg should have ½ inch holes, ½ inch deep drilled.

Then clean the spaces between the holes out with a chisel making sure you have a clean even slot to place the new wood in. Shape the new wood running the length of the grain on the wood and glue and clamp into place. Sand flush and finish.

(Fig. 16) A step by step process is shown at the end of this text.

Figure 15 A wood bit works very well as the point can be set on the line down the piece. Use a chisel to clean out the sides.

Figure 16 Spline has been glued in ready for final sanding.

Repairing Broken Dowel Ends – Step Down Dowels

Many times a stretcher, rung or turned piece will break off at the very end leaving a part in the joining piece. These are fixed using a process called a step down dowel. (Fig. 17)

First clean out the remaining broken dowel out of the piece, by drilling it out using smaller drill bits than the original dowel. Use the same method as in drilling out a broken dowel.

Take the rung, stretcher or turned piece and sand or file the end flat so that you can set a center point for drilling a hole no more than half the diameter of the piece you are drilling the hole in and about 2 inches deep. Then using dowel stock the same size as the broken dowel or larger if the exact size is not available, (commercial dowel stock is available at most hardware stores), I recommend oak or maple stock. Make a mark on the dowel rod the length of the new hole and proceed to sand or file the rod down so that the dowel fits tightly in the new hole. (Fig. 18) Using a pair of pliers squeeze grooves down the length of the new dowel. This allows the glue to move along the piece when glued in. Then measure the depth of the hole in the joining piece and cut the dowel to the overall length to join the two pieces back together. Glue the rung or turned end first, then when set, fit the whole piece back into the joining piece and continue gluing the piece. There are more examples at the end of the text.

Figure 17 A cut away dowel showing a step down dowel in place

Figure 18 The wood piece fits up into the hole and completes the back spindle.

Replacing Missing Parts or Pieces

Many times in furniture repair the turned pieces of legs, table bases or carvings, will come apart. These parts many times are originally glued together in the manufacturing process and then turned, shaped or carved to make the finished piece. (At the end of the text there are step by step photos for this process).

Another reason for this repair is, many times furniture is damaged to the point where the parts are missing, one of the biggest causes of this kind of damage are family pets chewing on the furniture.

If none of the parts are missing, you can simply glue them back on. In most cases the parts will be flat on the joining sides and should be dry fitted, to verify direction before applying glue. Sanding the flat areas first before applying the glue is a good idea, be sure to only remove glue, and keep the area flat. Then apply and thin layer of glue and clamp the piece in place. However; if the parts slide or move when glued, there are some other alternatives to clamping.

You can tape the part in place, using masking or duct tape.(Fig. 20) First hold the part in place applying gentle pressure for a minute or two, to give the glue a chance to bond. Then apply the tape over the area using as much pressure as the tape will bear without breaking.

Another method is to drill a pilot hole in the part being attached to the main piece. A pilot hole is a hole that is big enough to allow the screw to slide through the piece easily. Then hold the piece in place and drill another hole in the main piece using a drill bit smaller than the first, usually the size of the shaft of the screw being used. Then glue and screw into place tightly, but be careful not to tighten so as to split the wood. When the part is securely glued into place, remove the screw and putty the hole and touch up the part by sanding and applying the final color and finish.

When parts are completely missing there are various wood fillers, putties and epoxies that can be used to fill in or shape and color in. They have their place, but I have found that they never look quite right. They also can come out as the piece adjusts to changes in temperatures and humidity. So I repair the area using wood. I try to match color, grain and species of wood as much possible when doing this. The first step is to create a flat area on the damaged piece so as to be able to attach a new piece of wood to the damaged area . Chisels, sanding, wood files, all of these will get you a flat surface. The bigger and flatter the area, the stronger the glue bond to the new piece. (Fig. 19)

Figure 19 This piece broke during shipping.

Figure 19 The broken areas are filed flat, the new piece is cut.

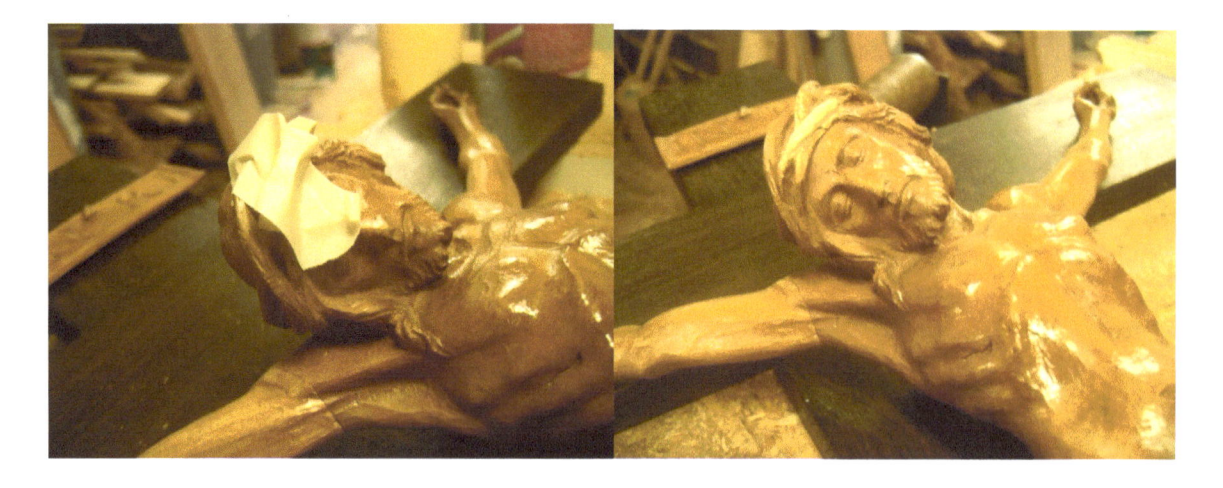

Figure 20 On irregular shapes masking taped hold parts until glue dries. Piece sanded into place, ready for touch up.

Next I pre-shape the new piece of wood being added as closely as possible to the desired end shape, leaving it over sized. When you have rough shaped the new piece, glue it into place. When it is secure, then you can start to shape the new piece to fit and blend with the existing piece. (Fig.20) I use my dremel with the sanding disk for this a lot, but wood files, sand paper, and chisels work also. I use the existing piece as a guide where the two pieces meet working my way out and around the new piece being fitted. Go slow and take time to study the part from different angles. When, the new piece is looking fitted, sand the final work into place feathering the new piece into the original part. Then apply the finishes required to blend the parts together. This is probably one of the most satisfying repairs I do, and if I take my time the end result is the piece is restored and doesn't look like anything ever happened to it.

Replacing or Repairing Veneer

For working with veneers, you need to add to you supplies waxed paper, contact cement and flat pieces of wood or metal plate to clamp over the top of the area old when the gluing is finished. Contact cement if standard in the industry for putting veneers down, however I have found that wood glue has enough moisture in it to make veneers pliable and when working with the warping that can happen in old veneers or in water damaged veneers the moisture from wood glue has let me rework those veneers very well.

If the veneer is chipped, split or lifted, but still in place, work glue under the edges with your finger until the glue is coming out around the surrounds areas. Push the piece back into place, wipe off any excess glue. Place the wax paper over the area, cover with the flat piece of wood or metal and clamp tightly into place. I recommend the wax paper, but if you use plastic be sure it is clear plastic without print, as the print can transfer to the veneer. Make sure everything is flat and there are no gaps around the wood or metal.

Figure 21 A table top where the veneer had lifted. A cut was made along the grain of the wood and glue injected in.

Figure 22 Appling even pressure using long boards and clamps.

If you are dealing with bubbles in the veneer, use a razor knife to cut a slit along the grain of the veneer, then using a syringe, inject glue into the bubble. (Fig.21) Then proceed to glue and clamp (Fig 22). I have used this method on table tops, cabinet sides, any place where the veneer has bubbled. When the glue is set and the clamps are removed, if necessary sand any raised areas flat and touch up. At the end of the text are a series of photos, step by step for this process. If pieces of veneer are missing, there are various fillers and epoxies that can be used to fill in the missing areas well as wood veneers.

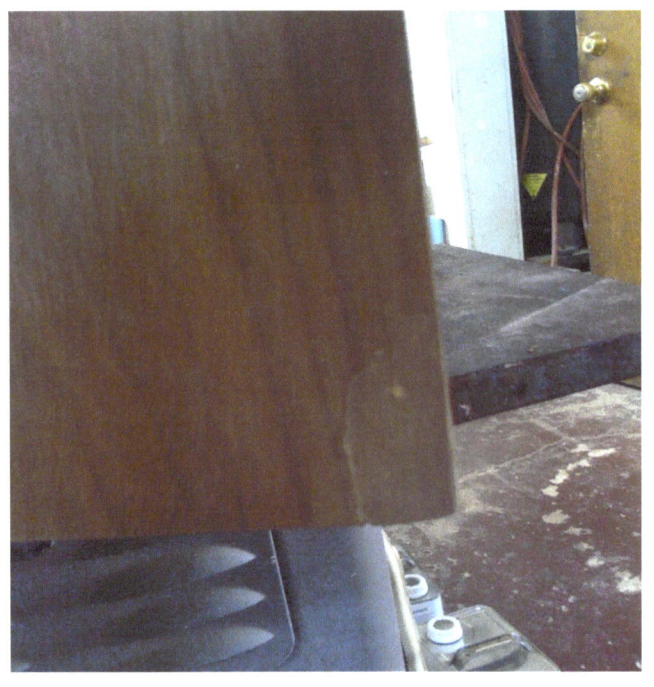

Figure 23 The missing veneer on the corner of the walnut chest has been filled in with walnut veneer and is ready for touch. At the end of the text are more step by step photos of this process.

First match as closely as possible the color of the wood and grain. Place a piece of paper over the area missing and do a pencil rubbing to gain a patterned image of the missing area. Cut out the pattern and mark it on the replacement veneer you have chosen. Check the paper pattern in the missing area for fit. Cut out the replacement piece using razor knife or scissors. Dry fit the two pieces together, if you are satisfied with the fit, then carefully sand a bevel around the edges where the two pieces will meet. If there are some gaps, don't worry about them they can be filled later with filler. Apply wood glue to the original piece, only in the area where the veneer is missing, fit in the new piece, then glue and clamp tightly. When the glue is set, remove the clamps, sand the areas flush and proceed to touch up. If the area where the missing veneer is deeper than the new veneer, you may have to cut several layers to fill in. With careful touch up this can be very successful. (Fig.23)

Tack Rails

Depending on how many times and piece has been upholstered, tack rails need to be repaired or replaced in order to give the fabric an area to be tacked to. Most of the time the rails can be filled, using a glue and saw dust mixture spread over the tacking area. Simply mix fine saw dust with wood glue into to paste, not runny but not dry either. Allow the mixture to dry and proceed to reupholster the piece.

The other method for tack rails is to make paper patters of the shape of the rails, cut out new wood pieces for replacing the broken rails. Remove the broken rails by using a small saw, chisel or sand the areas flat, then glue and screw the replacement pieces in.

Touch up of the finish

The first thing to keep in mind is safety and disposal of the products being used. Read all the manufactures labels and always work in areas with good ventilation, and wear gloves and protective clothing. This is the final stage to a good repair job and is probably the most important. If it is done right, the piece can look as if nothing has been done to it. In a standard reglue, many times the only thing necessary is simply wipe the piece down with a damp rag and make sure all the glue is off. If there are little chips, there are oils and polishes with color in them that can be wiped on to cover these areas. If more extensive work is needed, in an area where you have glued pieces back together, you sand those areas down smooth and flush with 120 to 150 grit sand paper. Fill the holes with good wood putty. (Fig. 24) Sometimes, a final sanding with 220 is necessary, but try working with the lesser grit paper first. The reason for not using the fine grit paper is you can polish the wood so that it will not accept the stain, and the finish will be lighter. Also when finish-sanding an area, you want to

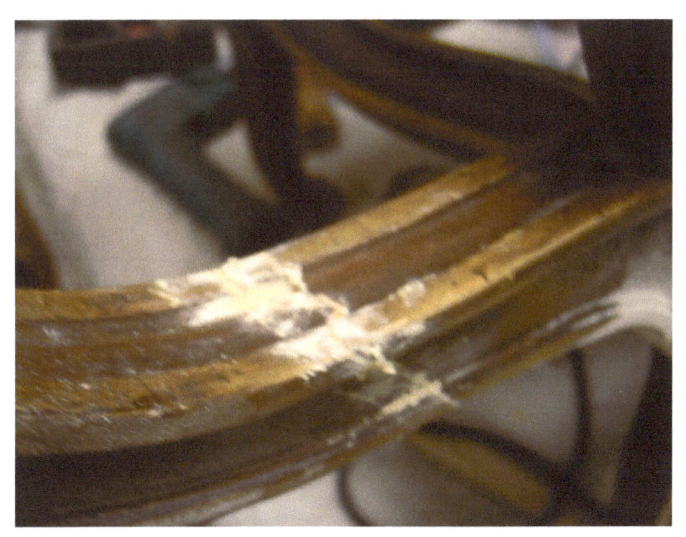

Figure 24 Note the uneven edges where the parts have been glued back together. The area has been filled with putty and is ready to be sanded smooth.

Figure 25 The original crack can be seen, but the area was sanded smooth and blended into the old finish. The dull color is the stain blended into the area. When the top coat is applied the area is shiny and not readily visible. When the stain is wet, that is what it will look like when top coated.

feather the area being sanded into the existing finish. (Fig. 25)

This will let you blend in the stain. There are several self-sealing stains on the market and hard finishes that go over the top. Color is important as most wood finishes are all made up of four basic colors with variations added to them to get the final color. Walnut colors, Cherry, Oak, Maple etc., all are basic browns that are a green brown, a red brown or a yellow-brown. The basic tints for these colors are raw umber, burnt umber, raw sienna and burnt sienna, then reds, blacks, blues, greens and yellows can be added to get the hues needed. In some cases white is also added. If you cannot decide what color is predominant on the piece, hold something next to the piece that is a primary color, and you will see the color in the piece reflect the basic color. Then you can choose a stain that will allow you to blend the area in right. In using commercial stains, it may take several coats applied over a period of time to achieve the depth of color necessary. Then when the stain is completely dry you will need a top coat. Most furniture has a lacquer top coat. There are spray lacquers on the market that are very good for going over the top and will allow you to blend in the finish. The first coat will feel rough, this is the sealing coat and when it is dry you need to lightly sand it smooth and reapply the top coat. Because spray finishes are lighter than brushed finishes, you may need to apply several coats. Also practice spraying on a piece of cardboard or wood first to get the feel for spraying. You want to avoid runs by just blasting away. Also be aware that there are several sheens available, but most furniture is usually gloss, semi-gloss or satin.

Do's and Don'ts

Don't take shortcuts unless you have previous experience. Much of what I do seems repetitive, but I found that rushing is usually when things go wrong. When I take my time, the job usually goes smoothly and I am more satisfied. I also build furniture and the things I have learned from my repairs have been very valuable to me.

Always glue the whole piece, otherwise, if the other joints are loose, with time and movement still being allowed to occur, at some point the whole piece will need to be done, and instead of an easy take apart and reglue, you have a chair, that has secure glued parts that won't let you take the rest apart. Also, if you have securely glued parts where there is no movement, don't take those joints apart. In trying to do so, you can split wood.

Always use wood glue, it is designed for wood, and if you need to take something apart again there are ways to do so. I have had to deal with epoxies and other types that don't bond the piece properly and ooze all over the outside of the piece and they become a nightmare to try to restore the finish. Wood glues are designed for wood, they bond with the wood, they have a certain amount of elasticity to them that moves with the expansion and contraction of the wood. They do require that the piece be clamped or secured for some time. But the set up time is getting less and less.

Additional Photos

Labeling

Note every piece is labeled and direction of rails is marked by the letters.

Clamping

This chair leg was split down the middle. Note the pieces of wood cut out to the shape of the leg so that the clamps can apply direct pressure.

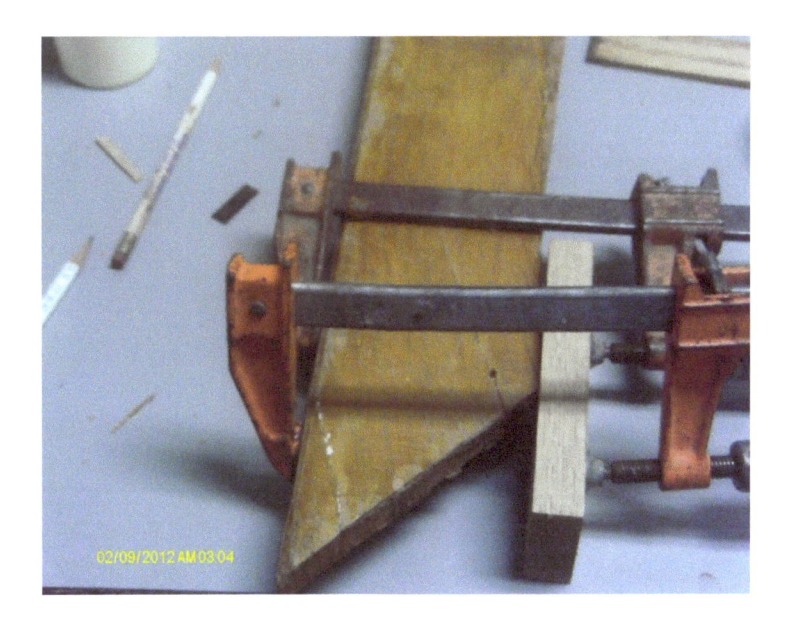

In order to clamp the split at the front of the rail, the straight piece of wood was clamped at the back first then at the front.

This piece is being glued in more than one direction. Notice the plastic between the board and the item being glued. It prevents the board from being glued to the piece as it is clamped into place to apply even pressure down the piece being glued.

This is a band clamp, a rope will work too. The rope can be tightened in the same way a tourniquet is applied in medical care.

Broken Dowel

Broken dowel

Broken dowel filed flush with flat area of leg small hole drilled in direction of dowel hole

Digging the old dowel out from wall of dowel hole

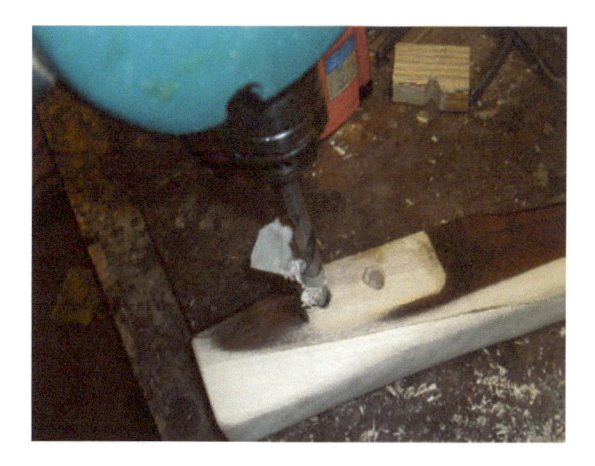

Once direction of original dowel hole is established, a correctly sized drill bit can finish cleaning out the hole

Glue Injection

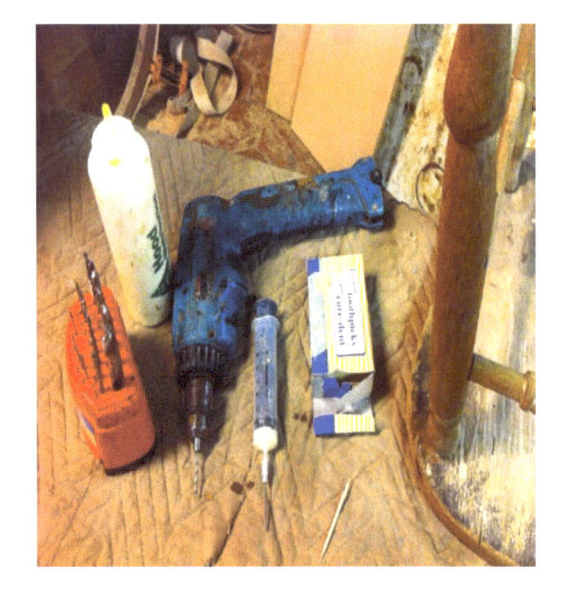

Tools needed

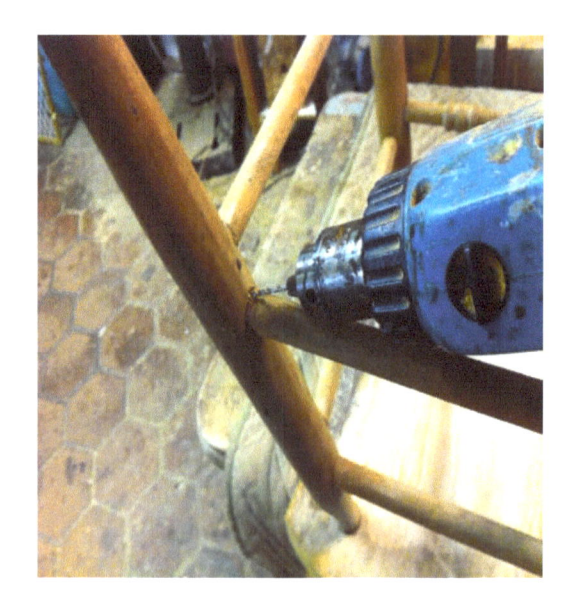

Drill small hole into pocket of joint

Using syringe inject glue into joint

Use tooth pick or small dowel to fill hole

Broken and Missing Parts

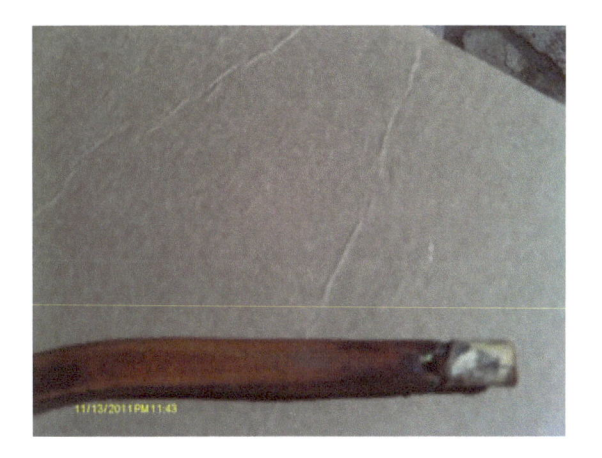

Damaged end on barrel chair arm.

A long cut is made, sanded flat in order to attach a new piece of wood

Once the new wood is glued into place, mark the rough outline of the basic shape to cut away

Final shaping with wood file and sand paper

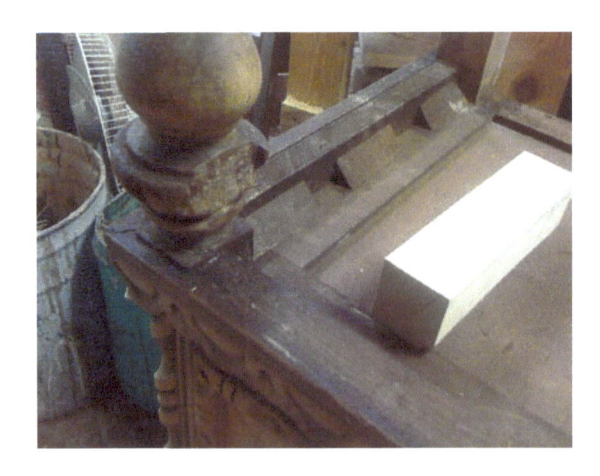

Missing piece was originally glued on

New piece fitted in place and marked for cutting

Clamping new piece in place

New piece of wood is sanded and filed into shape. Dremel is very useful

Finished Piece, the natural darks and lights of the wood when stained allow the new piece to be blended in.

Chair seat broken along glue joint

Biscuits inserted for alignment

Glued and clamped, clamp at front for top to bottom pressure

Reinforcement on bottom, glued and screwed into place

Step Down Dowel

The end of the club chair is too badly damaged to support the castor.

The metal cap is removed, and the old hole plugged with a dowel that goes past the area for the metal cap. The leg is now stabilized so that all parts where split are secure.

The leg is cut off at the place where the metal cap was placed. A hole was drilled for the new wood.

The new piece of wood has the reduced dowel made to go into the existing leg, and the other end in the shaped needed for the metal clamp.

Veneering

The area missing veneer has filled, and leveled below cabinet veneer, glued has been applied.

A veneer closely matched as possible is set into place

A metal plate (black under clamp head) is tightly clamped into place.

After clamping the piece is sanded down to meet the existing veneer. Ready for color blending and finishing.

Paper pattern made, to fit missing veneer

New veneer glued into place, note additional clamps, in order to get a tight clamping for new piece.

Clamps removed piece ready to be sanded to fit.

Piece sanded and fitted into place.

CPSIA information can be obtained
at www.ICGtesting.com
Printed in the USA
BVHW012204270223
659373BV00001B/1